HABITAT SURVIVAL

WETLANDS

Buffy Silverman

Chicago, Illinois

www.capstonepub.com
Visit our website to find out more information about Heinemann-Raintree books.

To order:
☎ Phone 800-747-4992

🖳 Visit www.capstonepub.com to browse our catalog and order online.

Edited by Nancy Dickmann, Kristen Kowalkowski, and Claire Throp
Designed by Philippa Jenkins
Original illustrations © Capstone Global Library Ltd 2013
Illustrations by Oxford Designers and Illustrators
Picture research by Tracy Cummins
Originated by Capstone Global Library Ltd
Printed and bound in the United States of America, North Mankato, MN

16 15 14 13 12
10 9 8 7 6 5 4 3 2

Library of Congress Cataloging-in-Publication Data
Silverman, Buffy.
  Wetlands / Buffy Silverman.
    p. cm.—(Habitat survival)
  Includes bibliographical references and index.
  ISBN 978-1-4109-4601-0 (hb)—ISBN 978-1-4109-4610-2 (pb) 1. Wetlands—Juvenile literature. I. Title.
  GB622.S55 2012
  577.68—dc23   2012000274

092012
006869RP

Acknowledgments
We would like to thank the following for permission to reproduce photographs: Corbis p. 26 (© moodboard), 28 (© Julie Dermansky/Corbis); Dreamstime p. 13 (© Jgaunion); FLPA pp. 6 (Robert Canis), 12 (Bob Gibbons), 16 (Konrad Wothe/Minden Pictures), 19 (Terry Whittaker), 21 (Bill Draker/Imagebroker), 27 (Theo Allofs/Minden Pictures); Getty Images pp. 17 (Enrique R. Aguirre Aves), 22 (Robert Nickelsberg/Liaison), 24 (Robin Bush), 25 (Roy Rainford/Robert Harding World Imagery); Nature Picture Library pp. 11 (Peter Cairns/2020VISION), 15 (Pete Oxford), 23 (Tim Laman); Shutterstock pp. 4 (© John Czenke), 5 (© Gerald A. DeBoer), 7 (© Diane Uhley), 8 (© Edwin Verin), 10 (© Leighton Photography & Imaging).

Cover photograph of a beaver feeding in a pond reproduced with permission of Photolibrary/Carey Alan & Sandy.

Every effort has been made to contact copyright holders of any material reproduced in this book. Any omissions will be rectified in subsequent printings if notice is given to the publisher.

Disclaimer
All the Internet addresses (URLs) given in this book were valid at the time of going to press. However, due to the dynamic nature of the Internet, some addresses may have changed, or sites may have changed or ceased to exist since publication. While the author and publisher regret any inconvenience this may cause readers, no responsibility for any such changes can be accepted by either the author or the publisher.

Contents

Some words are shown in bold, **like this**. You can find out what they mean by looking in the glossary.

What Is a Wetland?

A muskrat swims through shallow water, looking for the cattail plant's roots to eat. A hungry alligator swishes her tail and swims closer. Sensing danger, the muskrat disappears into a tunnel along the water's edge. Cattails, muskrat, and alligators live in the same **habitat**, called a wetland.

Soggy land

A wetland is land that is wet. If you watch the ground during a rainstorm you will see that rain soaks into spaces in the soil. When heavy rains fall, water puddles form on top. In a wetland, there is so much water that it fills all the spaces in soil. Then it floods the land.

Muskrat eat cattails and crabs that they find in a wetland.

Wetlands form in places where land and water meet, such as the edges of rivers, lakes, and the ocean. Some wetlands have **freshwater**, while others are salty. Some wetlands are always underwater, while others are wet only during certain seasons. There are wetlands all over the world, except in Antarctica.

Wetland homes

Wetlands are important habitats for many animals, including alligators, turtles, and snakes. **Migrating** birds rest in wetlands. Fish lay their eggs in calm waters.

Life in a Marsh

Marshes are a type of wetland. They form along the edges of lakes and rivers. Cattails and grasses grow in shallow marsh water. Pondweeds float in deeper water. Few trees grow in marshes.

In a marsh, water fills the soil, leaving no space for air. Marsh plant roots are **adapted** to grow in this waterlogged soil. Some of them get the air they need from above. Cattails have air spaces inside their stems. These air spaces make cattail stems strong and help them survive windstorms and floods.

A marsh harrier flies over reeds as it hunts for food.

River of grass

The Florida Everglades is one of the world's largest marshes. A shallow river flows slowly through huge saw grass fields. Wading birds, sea turtles, crocodiles, and manatees live here. The Everglades is home to some animals and plants that are found nowhere else in the world.

Land builders

The roots of marsh plants act like a net to trap dead leaves and stems. This **detritus** collects on plant roots. Detritus slowly **rots** and becomes part of the soil. Then new plants can grow in this rich soil. Animals come to feed and lay their eggs on the plants and detritus.

In a Swamp

A swamp is a wetland where trees and shrubs grow. Swamps form where slow-moving rivers and lakes flood the land. Swamp trees need air in their roots, but when the swamp floods there are no air spaces in the mucky soils. So cypress trees get air through "knees" that stick up like snorkels from the roots.

In the trees

Some swamp plants live high aboveground. Air plants, such as Spanish moss and ferns, grow on top of trees. Their roots collect rain and dew from the air.

Many animals live in a swamp. Fish, crayfish, tadpoles, and insects swim in swamp water. Forest animals, such as deer and bears, wade through swamps to find food. Great blue herons build nests in swamp trees. River otters have webbed feet and long bodies that are suited to slipping through the water.

Turtles warm their bodies in the Sun.

Giant wetland

Brazil's Pantanal is the world's largest wetland.
The Paraguay River flows through it. Low-lying
forests and marshes flood in the rainy season. The
Pantanal is home to thousands of kinds of plants and
animals, including butterflies, monkeys, crocodiles,
and macaws.

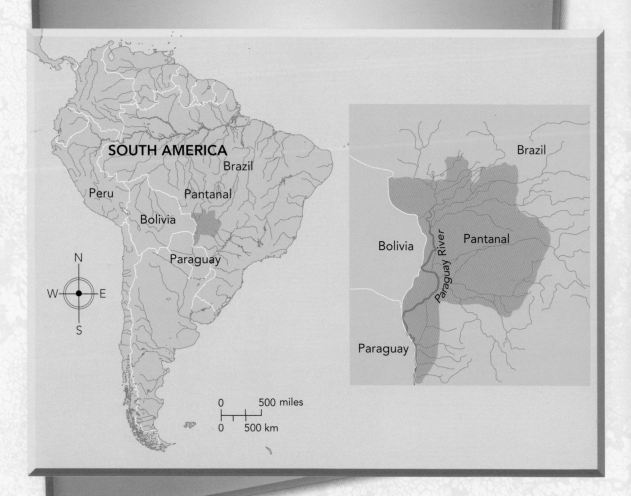

On a Bog

Bogs form in cool, wet places. Thick mats of squishy sphagnum moss grow over the brown water. In most **habitats**, **bacteria** break down dead plants and animals. But sphagnum moss holds a lot of water, leaving no space for air. Bacteria cannot fully break down dead matter in a waterlogged bog. When plants and animals die in a bog, they pile up. The bottom of the pile turns to **peat**. Peat is soggy, dead matter.

Bogs do not have the **nutrients** that plants need to grow. To survive, some bog plants trap and eat insects! Flies fall into the leafy tubes of a pitcher plant and drown in rainwater that collects inside. Then the plant breaks down the insects.

Insects drown in pitcher plants.

Many bogs have open water in the center, and floating moss around the edges.

Bog animals

Larger animals also live in bogs. Otters and badgers eat birds' eggs and chicks. In Ireland, red deer visit bogs to take a dip and get rid of flies.

Bog man

Many dead people have been found in bogs because bodies do not **rot** there. One man found in a bog in Denmark died more than 2,000 years ago. But you can still see his hair, fingernails, and skin.

At the Ocean's Edge

Salt marshes form along coasts, where land and seas meet. Twice a day, ocean **tides** rise and fall. During high tide, water floods a marsh. When the tide goes out, there is dry land. The tides bring **detritus**, or dead matter, to a marsh. Detritus and soil form a **mudflat** where grasses grow. Grass roots trap even more detritus, giving plants more space to grow.

Wave stoppers

Strong waves can hit salt marshes during storms. But the waves lose power as they wash across marshes. That stops them from harming coastlines.

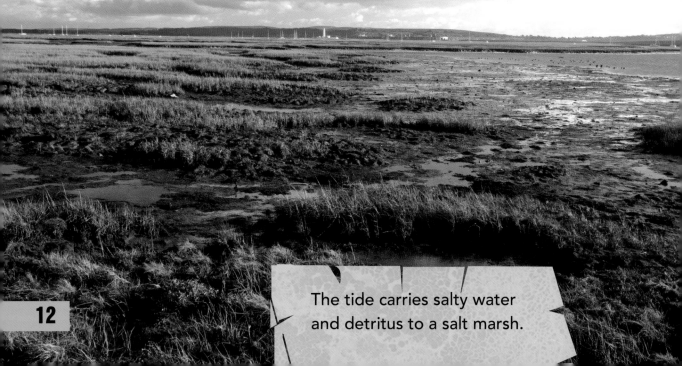

The tide carries salty water and detritus to a salt marsh.

Crabs pick up mud with their claws. They sift through it to find food.

Salt pumps

The tides bring saltwater into salt marshes, so plants there are **adapted** to get rid of extra salt. For example, cordgrass plants pump salt out of tiny holes in their leaves. Tides wash away the dry salt crystals.

Many animals live in tidal marshes. Fish lay their eggs in calm waters, then swim away. When the young fish hatch, they find plenty of food to eat. Crabs, snails, and worms burrow into mud and feed on detritus that washes over them.

Amazing Mangroves

Mangrove trees grow along **tropical** coasts. The **habitat** where they grow is called a mangrove swamp. During high **tide**, mangrove swamps are flooded with salty water. At low tide, the water disappears. Most kinds of trees cannot grow in wet, salty soil, but mangrove trees can.

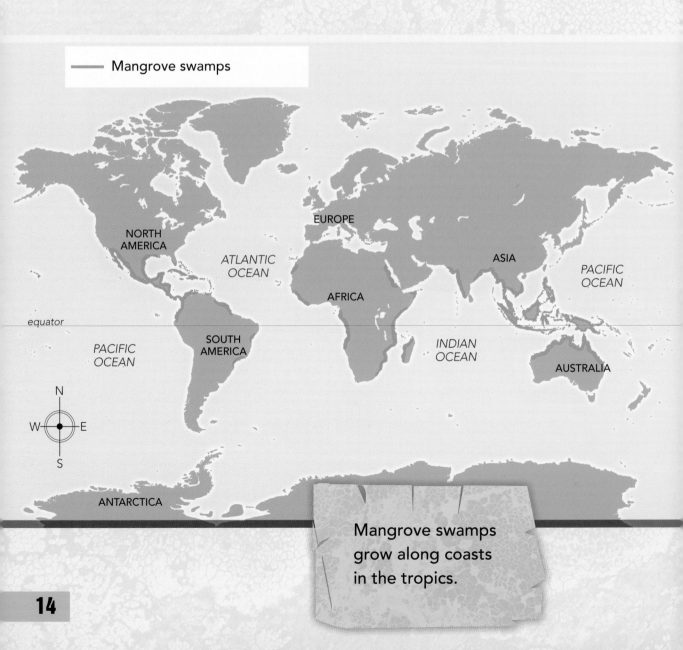

Mangrove swamps grow along coasts in the tropics.

Salt barriers

Red mangroves' roots **filter** water before they take it in. They keep salt out, but let in water. Black and white mangroves grow on higher ground. They take in salty water through their roots. Then they pump the salt out of their leaves.

Floating seedlings

Red mangrove seeds start to grow while still attached to a tree. A long, thin seedling drops from the tree and floats in water. Its roots grow while it floats. The seedling can survive this way for a year. Finally, when it reaches a sunny, muddy spot, its roots grow down.

Red mangroves look like they are walking on stilts. In fact, Native Americans called them walking trees. Their roots arch above water and some grow from branches. These spread-out roots prop trees up in muddy waters.

Red mangroves get air through roots above the water.

Mangrove Animals

Many different animals live among mangrove roots. The roots protect them from high winds and waves. They also trap dead leaves brought by the **tides**. After **bacteria** and **fungi** break this **detritus** down, the fish, shrimp, and crabs can eat it. Snails, barnacles, jellyfish, and sponges also find shelter in mangrove roots. Horseshoe crabs feed on many of these smaller animals.

Saltwater crocodiles hunt water buffalo in African mangrove swamps.

Mangrove swamps stop huge waves during a storm. This storm is taking place over coastal mangroves in Belize.

Fish nursery

Many fish lay their eggs among mangrove roots. The shallow water and tangled roots keep large **predators** away, so small fish can grow in safety.

Fishing cats hunt in Asian mangrove swamps. A fishing cat taps the water's surface with its paw, making ripples. Fish swim over, believing the ripples are from insects. Then the cat dives in and catches its dinner.

Tsunami stopper

Mangroves protect land from huge tidal waves, called tsunamis. When a big wave hits mangrove roots, it slows down. Most of the wave's **energy** is lost before it reaches land.

Freshwater Wetland Food Webs

Plants and animals in a wetland need each other to survive. They are connected by the flow of **energy**. All living things need energy to live and grow. They get energy from food. A food web shows how energy flows from one living thing to another.

Most food chains start with plants. Plants can use the Sun's energy to make their own food. **Freshwater** wetland plants, such as reeds and **algae**, make their own food in this way. Some animals get energy by eating plants. For example, water voles eat reeds. Snails and tadpoles eat algae.

Reeds, water voles, and marsh harriers are connected by the flow of energy in this food web.

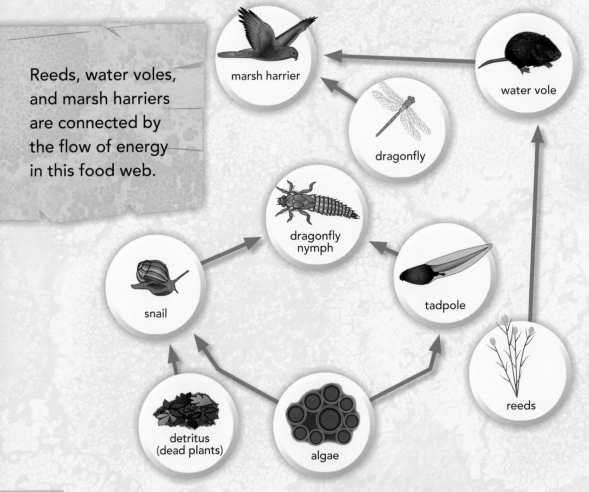

Water voles dig burrows in stream banks. They also weave ball-shaped nests on reed beds.

Predators

Predators are animals that get their energy by eating other animals. Young dragonflies live underwater and catch pond snails. Marsh harriers catch dragonflies and water voles.

All living things die, but their bodies still contain energy. **Bacteria** and **fungi** use that energy by breaking down dead plants and animals. This **detritus** feeds many wetland animals.

Shooting jaws

A dragonfly nymph's lower jaw is hinged. It folds up under its head. The jaw shoots out to capture **prey**.

Saltwater Wetland Food Webs

Plants and animals in a saltwater **habitat** also depend on each other. Thick strands of cordgrass grow in a salt marsh. Cordgrass uses the Sun's **energy** to make food in its leaf blades. It uses the energy to live and grow seeds.

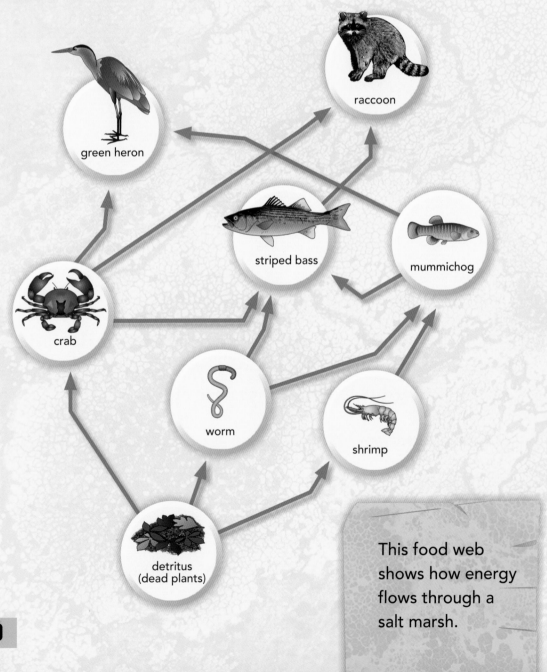

raccoon

green heron

striped bass

mummichog

crab

worm

shrimp

detritus
(dead plants)

This food web shows how energy flows through a salt marsh.

Puddle dining

Fiddler crabs feed on detritus, **algae**, and bacteria. But they don't like the sand and other bits that stick to detritus. They wash their food in puddles to separate the good parts from the bad.

Detritus eaters

Few animals eat cordgrass when it is alive, but many animals eat it after it dies. **Bacteria**, **fungi**, and other tiny organisms live on dead cordgrass. They turn it into **detritus**. Crabs, shrimp, worms, and growing insects feed on the detritus.

Small fish called mummichogs eat detritus, but they also eat shrimp and worms. Striped bass eat the mummichogs and other small fish, as well as crabs. Raccoons catch crabs and fish.

This raccoon wades in a salt marsh to catch crayfish.

Wetlands in Trouble

Wetlands around the world are in trouble. More than half of the world's wetlands have disappeared in the past 100 years. People change wetlands in many ways. They drain wetlands to grow food. They build **dams** that change water flow and dig **channels** to control floods.

Many cities now stand on land that used to be wetland. When water with chemicals from farms and factories reaches wetlands, it can harm plants and animals. The chemicals make water unsafe for people, too.

Wetlands are drained to make room for houses.

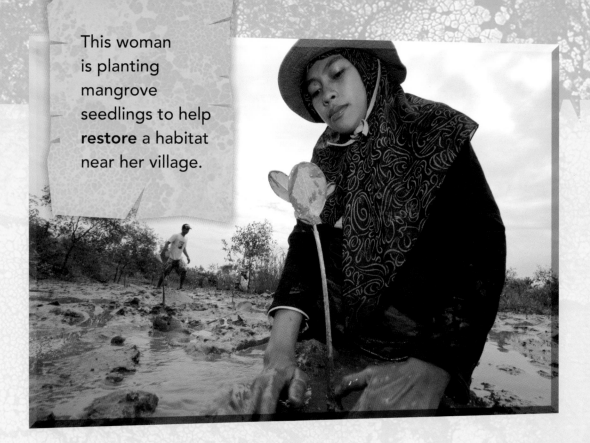

This woman is planting mangrove seedlings to help **restore** a habitat near her village.

Mangrove decline

People sometimes think of swamps as smelly, useless places. Mangrove swamps are one of the **tropical habitats** most in danger. Half of the mangrove swamps in many Asian countries have disappeared. People clear mangroves to make room for farms, cities, and harbors.

Saving swamps

Many people realize that mangrove swamps help humans by protecting land from storms. The mangroves are also important habitats for birds, fish, and other animals. Governments have passed laws to protect mangroves. Groups work to keep these habitats safe.

Disappearing Bogs and Fens

Peat can be burned to heat homes, or added to garden soil to help plants grow. For thousands of years, people have dug peat from bogs. But peat takes a long time to form. If we dig too much, too quickly, the bog doesn't have time to recover. Some bogs have also been drained so that the land can be used for other purposes.

Some Irish bogs are getting a second chance. People are removing drains and taking out trees and other plants. Then bog plants can grow again.

Blocks of peat are harvested from an Irish bog.

The great fen

A fen is a low-lying wetland. Some English farmlands are being returned to fens. Many groups are working to **restore** a large fen. The planned fen will join two nature **reserves**.

People plan to expand this small fen in England.

Fens into farms

Fens once covered a large area of eastern England. The **freshwater** and salt marshes that made up fens often flooded, so only higher areas could be farmed. People fished and hunted in fens. Then, many years ago, people began draining the fens. Once the land no longer flooded, it could be farmed.

Protecting Marshes and Swamps

Around the world, people are concerned about wetlands. They know that animals need wetland **habitats**. Marshes and swamps provide food, shelter, and a place for young animals to grow. To protect animals, we must protect their habitats.

The rare Cuban crocodile lives in the Zapata Swamp in Cuba. The swamp is one of the largest wetlands remaining in the Caribbean. It is also the largest protected area in Cuba. Scientists are studying the crocodile and its habitat. They want to make sure the crocodile survives.

People, animals, and plants benefit when wetlands are protected.

Monkeys and more

Tanjung Puting National Park in Indonesia is home to rare plants and animals. The park protects **peat** swamp forests, mangrove forests, and other wetlands. It also protects many rare animals. Orangutans, proboscis monkeys, butterflies, and waterbirds live in the park.

Helping ourselves

Wetlands can help people, too. They slow floodwaters, saving people's lives and property. Wetlands clean **pollutants** from water. They give us a place to hike, canoe, and watch wildlife. Governments in many countries pass laws to protect wetlands. Laws can stop people from draining more wetlands. They help save the wetlands that remain.

Protecting Coastal Wetlands

Tidal marshes all over the world are disappearing, but many people are trying to bring them back. For example, the Blackwater National Wildlife Refuge in Maryland has been losing marshland for years. Scientists have a plan to **restore** the tidal marshes by digging up dirt and **detritus** from river bottoms. They pump the detritus into washed-out marshes and plant marsh grass in the muck. As the grasses die, detritus piles up and enriches the soil, so more plants can grow. Animals also come to eat the detritus.

All of us can help protect wetlands by keeping them clean.

Wetland Watchers

Scientists are not the only ones saving wetlands. Kids in Louisiana care for wetlands, too. A Louisiana teacher started Wetland Watchers in 1998. Students in Wetland Watchers adopted 28 acres of tidal wetland. Thousands of students have learned about wetlands while helping to care for them. The students remove trash and plant trees. They test the water to see if it is clean. They also built a nature trail that visitors enjoy.

You can help wetlands!

Here are some ways that you can help wetlands:

- Find out more about them—read books and research web sites.
- Visit wetlands near your home to learn about the plants and animals that live there.
- Join a conservation group that protects wetland species.
- Be **energy** wise to help reduce **global warming**.
- Tell your friends and family so they can help, too.

Glossary

adapt change that helps a plant or animal survive in a particular place

algae very simple plants that mainly live in water

bacteria single-celled organism that breaks down dead matter

channel long, narrow groove in the ground where water runs

dam barrier made to hold back water in a river. The dam causes the water level to rise.

detritus debris from decaying organisms

energy power needed to grow, move, and live

fen low-lying, flat, shallow wetland

filter separate and remove matter that is in a liquid

freshwater water that is not salty

fungi group of organisms that breaks down dead matter. Yeasts, molds, and mushrooms are fungi.

global warming increase in Earth's temperature, caused by chemicals in the air that trap the Sun's heat

habitat place where a plant or animal lives

migrate move from one location to another

mudflat low-lying, muddy land that is covered with water at high tide and exposed at low tide

nutrient chemical that plants and animals need to live

peat partially decayed plant matter formed in a bog. Peat is used for fuel and fertilizer.

pollutant chemical that is harmful to air, water, or land

predator animal that hunts and eats other animals

prey animal that is hunted and eaten by another animal

reserve part of the land that is protected

restore bring something back to its original condition

rot break down due to the action of bacteria or fungi

tide rise and fall of sea level caused by the pull of the Moon

tropical area on either side of the equator, where the weather is always warm

Find Out More

Books

Hodge, Deborah. *Who Lives Here? Wetland Animals.* Toronto: Kids Can Press, 2008.

Kurtz, Kevin. *A Day in the Salt Marsh.* Mount Pleasant, S.C.: Sylvan Dell Publishing, 2007.

Salas, Laura Purdie. *Wetlands: Soggy Habitat.* Mankato, Minn.: Picture Window Books, 2007.

Wechsler, Doug. *Marvels in the Muck: Life in the Salt Marshes.* Honesdale, Pa.: Boyds Mills Press, 2008.

Internet Sites

Facthound offers a safe, fun way to find Internet sites related to this book. All of the sites on Facthound have been researched by our staff.

Here's all you do:

Visit *www.facthound.com*

Type in this code: 9781410946010

Index